THE
Heart *of*
Understanding

THE
Heart *of*
Understanding

COMMENTARIES *on* *the* PRAJÑAPARAMITA HEART SUTRA

Thich Nhat Hanh
EDITED BY Peter Levitt

~

PARALLAX PRESS
Berkeley, California

Parallax Press
P.O. Box 7355
Berkeley, California 94707
www.parallax.org

Parallax Press is the publishing division of
Unified Buddhist Church, Inc.

Cover design by Robin Terra.
Text design by Madonna Gauding.
Author photo by Richard Friday.
Printed in Canada.

Library of Congress Cataloging-in-Publication Data.

Nhât Hanh, Thích.
The heart of understanding : commentaries on the Prajñaparamita Heart
Sutra / Thich Nhat Hanh ; edited by Peter Levitt. -- [Rev. ed.]
      p. cm.
ISBN 978-1-888375-92-3
1. Tripitaka. Sutrapitaka. Prajñaparamita. Hrdaya--Commentaries. I. Levitt,
Peter. II. Tripitaka. Sutrapitaka. Prajñaparamita. Hrdaya. English. III. Title.
BQ1967.N48 2009
294.3'85--dc22

                                    2009027146

2 3 4 5 / 13 12 11 10

CONTENTS ~

FOREWORD ~

The Prajñaparamita Heart Sutra is the essence of Buddhist teaching. It is chanted or recited daily in monastic and lay communities throughout the world. Thich Nhat Hanh's commentaries, contained in this book, are part of the continuous stream of oral transmission basic to Buddhism since the time of Shakyamuni Buddha, 2,500 years ago. The literature of the Prajñaparamita (Perfect Understanding) dates back to the beginning of the Christian Era and has been studied and expounded for 2,000 years, first in India, and then in China, Japan, Vietnam, Korea, Tibet, and other countries with a Mahayana Buddhist tradition.

For nearly a century, these teachings have been available in English, and for more than fifty years they have been taught in the West in the context of meditation practice by Zen and Tibetan teachers. Often, these teachings have proven difficult for Westerners to understand.

In the spring of 1987, Vietnamese Zen master, poet, and activist for peace Thich Nhat Hanh offered a series of retreats and lectures in California, the Pacific Northwest, Colorado, New England, and New York. He encouraged his American listeners to join him in an experiment to discover what he called "the true face of American Buddhism," one that is not foreign but springs from the depths of our understanding. "Buddhism is not one. The teachings of Buddhism are many. When Buddhism enters a country, that country always acquires a new form of Buddhism. . . . The teaching of Buddhism in this country will be different from other countries. Buddhism, in order to be Buddhism, must be suitable, appropriate to the psychology and the culture of the society that it serves." To enrich our understanding and aid us in our explorations, Thay (an informal title for "teacher," pronounced "tie") offered several talks on the Prajñaparamita Heart Sutra. Some of these were public lectures delivered to seven or eight hundred listeners, and others were offered to fifty or sixty people on retreat together.

At the retreat in Ojai, California, artists and meditators sat beneath a large oak in the cradle of the Los Padres Mountains, the sound of early morning birds or the touch of a warm breeze accompanying Thay's gentle, penetrating voice. His talks on the Heart Sutra were singularly comprehensible, bringing new life and vivid understanding to this ancient teaching. This book is a compilation of several of those talks, several streams flowing together to form one.

During the retreats, Thay encouraged participants to give calm, clear-seeing, and intimate attention to each daily activity, whether eating a meal, drawing a Buddha, or just walking quietly, aware of the contact between our foot and the earth that supports it. In order to encourage this kind of mindfulness, a bell master sounded a large bell regularly, and everyone stopped their activity, breathed three times, and recited silently, "Listen, listen, this wonderful sound brings me back to my true self."

"A bell is a bodhisattva," Thay said. "It helps us to wake up." With this in mind, when the bell was invited to sound we put down our garden tools, our hammers, our paint brushes or pens, and came back to ourselves for a moment, breathing with a natural serenity, smiling a relaxed smile to ourselves and all those around us—the people, the trees, a flower, a child running with delight, even our worries and sometimes our pain. As we did this, we just listened deeply and became one with the sound of the bell. It is truly remarkable how deeply a bell can ring inside a person. After this pause, we resumed our activity with renewed energy, a little more attentively, a little more aware.

A bell is not the only kind of bodhisattva. Anything can help us to awaken to the present moment and all that it contains. "Buddhism is a clever way to enjoy life," Thay says. In this light, I would like to suggest you read this small book as if listening to a bell. Put down your daily tasks for a moment, both physical and mental, sit comfortably, and allow the words of this wonderful teacher to ring deeply inside you. I am certain, if you bring yourself and this book together in this way, you will hear the bell of mindfulness many times. When it rings, lower the book and listen to its sound echoing in your own depths. You might even try breathing calmly and offering a smile. This may seem difficult at first, as it did for many of us, but I can still hear

Thay's encouraging voice tell us, "You can do it!" In this way, the depth of your heart and of the Heart Sutra will come very close. They might even touch.

Intimacy is at the heart of the teaching contained in this book. In the thirteenth century, Zen Master Eihei Dogen taught that enlightenment is just intimacy with all things. Thich Nhat Hanh's teaching is the same. When we allow the true heart of understanding to arise within us, such intimacy is not only possible, it is the spontaneous expression of what we and all things truly are. To allow our lives to be guided by such intimacy is to nourish the seed of compassion within us and others alike. Peace between partners, neighbors, nations—even peace within ourselves—may sometimes seem an impossible dream, but if we look deeply into the heart of the teaching Thich Nhat Hanh offers, I think we can discover a way for such peace to be realized. Peace in our world is not far from there.

Peter Levitt
Salt Spring Island
British Columbia
June 2009

THE HEART OF PERFECT UNDERSTANDING

The Bodhisattva Avalokita,
while moving in the deep course of Perfect Understanding,
shed light on the Five Skandhas and found them equally empty.
After this penetration, he overcame ill-being.

"Listen, Shariputra,
form is emptiness, and emptiness is form.
Form is not other than emptiness, emptiness is not other than form.
The same is true with feelings, perceptions, mental formations, and
      consciousness.

"Listen, Shariputra, all dharmas are marked with emptiness.
They are neither produced nor destroyed,
neither defiled nor immaculate,
neither increasing nor decreasing.
Therefore, in emptiness there is neither form, nor feelings, nor
      perceptions,
nor mental formations, nor consciousness.
No eye, or ear, or nose, or tongue, or body, or mind.
No form, no sound, no smell, no taste, no touch, no object of mind.
No realms of elements (from eyes to mind-consciousness),
no interdependent origins and no extinction of them
(from ignorance to death and decay).

No ill-being, no cause of ill-being, no end of ill-being, and
no path.
No understanding and no attainment.

"Because there is no attainment,
the Bodhisattvas, grounded in Perfect Understanding,
find no obstacles for their minds.
Having no obstacles, they overcome fear,
liberating themselves forever from illusion, realizing perfect
Nirvana.
All Buddhas in the past, present, and future,
thanks to this Perfect Understanding,
arrive at full, right, and universal Enlightenment.

"Therefore, one should know
that Perfect Understanding is the highest mantra, the
unequalled mantra,
the destroyer of ill-being, the incorruptible truth.
A mantra of Prajñaparamita should therefore be proclaimed:
Gate gate paragate parasamgate bodhi svaha."*

*Gone, gone, gone all the way over, everyone gone to the other
shore, enlightenment, hurrah!

INTERBEING ～

I f you are a poet, you will see clearly that there is a cloud floating in this sheet of paper. Without a cloud, there will be no rain; without rain, the trees cannot grow; and without trees, we cannot make paper. The cloud is essential for the paper to exist. If the cloud is not here, the sheet of paper cannot be here either. So we can say that the cloud and the paper *inter-are*. "Interbeing" is a word that is not in the dictionary yet, but if we combine the prefix "inter-" with the verb "to be," we have a new verb, *inter-be*.

If we look into this sheet of paper even more deeply, we can see the sunshine in it. If the sunshine is not there, the forest cannot grow. In fact, nothing can grow. Even we cannot grow without sunshine. And so, we know that the sunshine is also in this sheet of paper. The paper and the sunshine inter-are. And if we continue to look, we can see the logger who cut the tree and brought it to the mill to be transformed into paper. And we see the wheat. We know that the logger cannot exist without his daily bread, and therefore the wheat that became his bread is also in this sheet of paper. And the logger's father and mother are in it too. When we look in this way, we see that without all of these things, this sheet of paper cannot exist.

Looking even more deeply, we can see we are in it too. This is not difficult to see, because when we look at a sheet of paper, the sheet of paper is part of our perception. Your mind is in here and mine is also. So we can say that everything is in here in this sheet of paper. You cannot point out one thing that is not here—time, space, the earth, the rain, the minerals in the soil, the sunshine, the cloud, the river, the heat. Everything coexists with this sheet of paper. That is why I think the word inter-be should be in the dictionary. To be is to inter-be. You cannot just *be* by yourself alone. You have to inter-be with every other thing. This sheet of paper is, because everything else is.

Suppose we try to return one of the elements to its source. Suppose we return the sunshine to the sun. Do you think that this sheet of paper would be possible? No, without sunshine nothing can be. And if we return the logger to his mother, then we have no sheet of paper either. The fact is that this sheet of paper is made up only of "non-paper elements." And if we return these non-paper elements to their sources, then there can be no paper at all. Without non-paper elements, like mind, logger, sunshine, and so on, there will be no paper. As thin as this sheet of paper is, it contains everything in the universe in it.

But the Heart Sutra seems to say the opposite. Avalokiteshvara tells us that things are empty. Let us look more closely.

EMPTY OF WHAT? ~

The Bodhisattva Avalokita,
while moving in the deep course of Perfect Understanding,
shed light on the Five Skandhas and found them equally empty.

odhi means being awake, and *sattva* means a living being, so *bodhisattva* means an awakened being. All of us are sometimes bodhisattvas, and sometimes not. Avalokita is the shorter name of the bodhisattva Avalokiteshvara. Avalokita is neither male nor female and sometimes appears as a man and sometimes as a woman. In Chinese, Vietnamese, Korean, and Japanese, this bodhisattva's name is sometimes translated as Guanyin, Quan Am, Gwaneum, and Kannon, which means "the one who listens and hears the cries of the world in order to come and help." Avalokiteshvara also embodies the spirit of non-fear, as he himself has transcended fear. The Prajñaparamita Heart Sutra is his wonderful gift to us.

Perfect Understanding is *prajñaparamita* in Sanskrit. The word "wisdom" is usually used to translate *prajña,* but I think that wisdom is somehow not able to convey the meaning. Understanding is like water flowing in a stream. Wisdom and knowledge are solid and can block our understanding. In Buddhism, knowledge is regarded as an obstacle for understanding. If we take something to be the truth, we may cling to it so much that even if the truth comes and knocks at our door, we won't want to let it in. We have to be able to transcend our previous knowledge in the same way we climb up a ladder. If we are on the fifth rung and think that we are very high, there is no hope for us to step up to the sixth. We must learn to transcend our own views. Understanding, like water, can flow, can penetrate. Views, knowledge, and even wisdom are solid, and can block the way of understanding.

According to Avalokiteshvara, this sheet of paper is empty; but according to our analysis, it is full of everything. There seems to be a contradiction between our observation and his. Avalokita found the five skandhas empty. But, empty of what? The key word is *empty*. To be empty is to be empty of something.

If I am holding a cup of water and I ask you, "Is this cup empty?" you will say, "No, it is full of water." But if I pour out the water and ask you again, you may say, "Yes, it is empty." But empty of what? Empty means empty of something. The cup cannot be empty of nothing. "Empty" doesn't mean anything unless you know "empty of what?" My cup is empty of water, but it is not empty of air. To be empty is to be *empty of something*. This is quite a discovery. When Avalokita says that the five skandhas are equally empty, to help him be precise we must ask, "Mr. Avalokita, empty of what?"

The five skandhas, which may be translated into English as five heaps, or five aggregates, are the five elements that comprise a human being. These five elements flow like a river in every one of us. In fact, these are really five rivers flowing together in us: the river of form, which means our body; the river of feelings; the river of perceptions; the river of mental formations; and the river of consciousness. They are always flowing in us. So according to Avalokita, when he looked deeply into the nature of these five rivers, he suddenly saw that all five are empty.

And if we ask, "Empty of what?" he has to answer. And this is what he said: "They are empty of a separate self." That means none of these five rivers can exist by itself alone. Each of the five rivers has to be made by the other four. It has to coexist; it has to inter-be with all the others.

In our bodies we have lungs, heart, kidneys, stomach, and blood. None of these can exist independently. They can only coexist with the others. Your lungs and your blood are two things, but neither can exist separately. The lungs take in air and enrich the blood, and, in turn, the blood nourishes the lungs. Without the blood, the lungs cannot be alive, and without the lungs, the blood cannot be cleansed. Lungs and blood inter-are. The same is true with kidneys and blood, kidneys and stomach, lungs and heart, blood and heart, and so on.

When Avalokita says that our sheet of paper is empty, he means it is empty of a separate, independent existence. It cannot just be by itself. It has to inter-be with the sunshine, the cloud, the forest, the logger, the mind, and everything else. It is empty of a separate self. But, empty of a separate self means full of everything. So it seems that our observation and that of Avalokita do not contradict each other after all.

Avalokita looked deeply into the five skandhas of form, feelings, perceptions, mental formations, and consciousness, and he discovered that none of them can be by itself alone. Each can only inter-be with all the others. So he tells us that form is empty. Form is empty of a separate self, but it is full of everything in the cosmos. The same is true with feelings, perceptions, mental formations, and consciousness.

THE WAY OF UNDERSTANDING ~

After this penetration, he overcame ill-being.

Penetration means to enter something, not just to stand outside of it. When we want to understand something, we cannot just stand outside and observe it. We have to enter deeply into it and be one with it in order to really understand. If we want to understand a person, we have to feel their feelings, suffer their sufferings, and enjoy their joy. The sutra uses the word "penetration" to mean "full comprehension." The word "comprehend" is made up of the Latin roots *com,* which means "together in mind," and *prehendere,* which means "to grasp it or pick it up." So to comprehend something means to pick it up and be one with it. There is no other way to understand something.

If we only look at the sheet of paper as an observer, standing outside, we cannot understand it completely. We have to penetrate it. We have to *be* a cloud, *be* the sunshine, and *be* the logger. If we can enter it and be everything that is in it, our understanding of the sheet of paper will be perfect.

There is an Indian story about a grain of salt that wanted to know just how salty the ocean was, so it jumped in and became one with the water of the ocean. In this way, the grain of salt gained perfect understanding.

If we are concerned with peace and want to understand another country, we can't just stand outside and observe. We have to be one with a citizen of that country in order to understand her feelings, perceptions, and mental formations. Any meaningful work for peace must follow the principle of nonduality, the principle of penetration. This is our peace practice: to penetrate, to be one with, in order to really understand.

In the Sutra on the Four Foundations of Mindfulness, the Buddha recommended that we observe in a penetrating way. He said we should contemplate the body *in* the body, the feelings *in* the feelings, the mental formations *in* the mental formations. Why did he use this kind of repetition? Because you have to enter in order to be one with what you want to observe and understand. Nuclear scientists are beginning to say this also. When you enter the world of elementary particles you have to become a participant in order to understand something. You can no longer stand outside and remain just an observer. Today many scientists prefer the word "participant" to the word "observer."

In our effort to understand each other we should do the same. A husband and wife who wish to understand each other have to be in the skin of their partner in order to feel, otherwise they cannot really understand. In the light of Buddhist meditation, love is impossible without understanding. You cannot love someone if you do not understand him or her. If you don't understand and you love, that is not love; it is something else.

Avalokita's meditation was a deep penetration into the five skandhas. Seeing deeply into the rivers of form, feelings, perceptions, mental formations, and consciousness, he discovered the empty nature of all of them, and suddenly, he overcame all pain. All of us who would like to arrive at that kind of emancipation will have to look deeply in order to penetrate the true nature of emptiness.

LONG LIVE EMPTINESS ∼

"Listen, Shariputra,
form is emptiness, and emptiness is form.
Form is not other than emptiness, emptiness is not other than form.
The same is true with feelings, perceptions, mental formations,
*   and consciousness.*

Form is the wave and emptiness is the water. To understand this, we have to think differently than many of us who were raised in the West were trained to think. In the West, when we draw a circle, we consider it to be zero, nothingness. But in India and many other Asian countries, a circle means totality, wholeness. The meaning is the opposite. So "form is emptiness, and emptiness is form" is like wave is water, water is wave. "Form is not other than emptiness, emptiness is not other than form. The same is true with feelings, perceptions, mental formations, and consciousness," because these contain each other. Because one exists, everything exists.

In the Vietnamese literary canon, there are two lines of poetry by a twelfth-century Zen master of the Ly dynasty that say:

If the cosmos exists, then the smallest speck of dust exists.
If the smallest speck of dust doesn't exist, then the
  whole cosmos doesn't exist.

The poet means that the notions of existence and nonexistence are just created by our minds. He also said that "the entire cosmos can be put on the tip of a hair," and "the sun and the moon can be seen in a mustard seed." These images show us that one contains everything, and everything is just one.

Because form is emptiness, form is possible. In form we find everything else—feelings, perceptions, mental formations, and consciousness. "Emptiness" means empty of a separate self. It is full of everything, full of life. The word "emptiness" should not scare us. It is a wonderful word. To be empty does not mean to be nonexistent. If the sheet of paper is not empty, how could the sunshine, the logger, and the forest come into it? How could it be a sheet of paper? The cup, in order to be empty, has to be there. Form, feelings, perceptions, mental formations, and consciousness, in order to be empty of a separate self, have to be there.

Emptiness is the ground of everything. "Thanks to emptiness, everything is possible." That is a declaration made by Nagarjuna, a Buddhist philosopher of the second century. Emptiness is quite an optimistic concept. If I am not empty, I cannot be here. And if you are not empty, you cannot be there. Because you are there, I can be here. This is the true meaning of emptiness. Form does not have a separate existence. Avalokita wants us to understand this point.

If we are not empty, we become a block of matter. We cannot breathe, we cannot think. To be empty means to be alive, to breathe in and to breathe out. We cannot be alive if we are not empty. Emptiness is impermanence, it is change. We should not complain about impermanence, because without impermanence nothing is possible. A Buddhist who came to see me from Great Britain complained that life was empty and impermanent. (He had been a Buddhist for five years and had thought about emptiness and impermanence a great deal.) He told me that one day his fourteen-year-old daughter told him, "Daddy, please don't complain about impermanence. Without impermanence, how can I grow up?" Of course she was right.

When you have a kernel of corn and you entrust it to the soil, you hope that it will become a tall corn plant. If there is no impermanence, the kernel of corn will remain a kernel of corn forever and you will never have an ear of corn to eat. Impermanence is crucial to the life of everything. Instead of complaining about impermanence, we might say, "Long live impermanence!" Thanks to impermanence, everything is possible. That is a very optimistic note. And it is the same with emptiness. Emptiness is important because without emptiness, nothing is possible. So we should also say, "Long live emptiness!" Emptiness is the basis of everything. Thanks to emptiness, life itself is possible. All the five skandhas follow this same principle.

HAPPY CONTINUATION ~

"Listen, Shariputra, all dharmas are marked with emptiness.
They are neither produced nor destroyed.

"D harmas" in this line means "things." A human being
is a dharma. A tree is a dharma. A cloud is a dharma.
The sunshine is a dharma. Everything that can be conceived
of is a dharma. So when we say, "All dharmas are marked
with emptiness," we are saying, "Everything has emptiness
as its own nature." And that is why everything can be. There
is a lot of joy in this statement. It means nothing can be born,
nothing can die. Avalokita has said something extremely
important.

Every day in our life, we see birth and we see death.
When a person is born, a birth certificate is printed for
them. After they die, a death certificate is made. These
certificates confirm the existence of birth and death. But
Avalokita said, "No, there is no birth and death." We have
to look more deeply to see whether his statement is true.

What is the date on which you were born, your birth
date? Before that date, did you already exist? Were you
already there before you were born? Let me help you. To
be born means from nothing you become something. My
question is, before you were born, were you already there?

Suppose a hen is about to lay an egg. Before she gives birth, do you think the egg is already there? Yes, of course. It is inside. You also were inside before you were outside. That means that before you were born, you already existed—inside your mother. The fact is that if something is already there, it does not need to be born. To be born means from nothing you become something. If you are already something, what is the use of being born?

So, your so-called birthday is really your Continuation Day. The next time you celebrate, you can say, "Happy Continuation Day." I think that we may have a better concept of when we were born. If we go back nine months to the time of our conception, we have a better date to put on our birth certificates. In China, and also in Vietnam, when you are born, you are already considered one year old. So we say we begin to be at the time of our conception in our mother's womb, and we write down that date on our birth certificate.

But the question remains: Even before that date, did you exist or not? If you say, "Yes," I think you are correct. Before your conception, you were there already, maybe half in your father, half in your mother. Because from nothing, we can never become something. Can you name one thing that was once a nothing? A cloud? Do you think that a cloud can be born out of nothing? Before becoming a cloud, it was water, maybe flowing as a river. It was not nothing. Do you agree?

We cannot conceive of the birth of anything. There is only continuation. Please look back even further and you will see that you not only exist in your father and mother, but you also exist in your grandparents and your great-grandparents. As I look more deeply, I can see that in a former life I was a cloud. This is not poetry; it is science. Why do I say that in a former life I was a cloud? Because I am still a cloud. Without the cloud, I cannot be here. I am the cloud, the river, and the air at this very moment, so I know that in the past I have been a cloud, a river, and the air. And I was a rock. I was the minerals in the water. This is not a question of belief in reincarnation. This is the history of life on Earth. We have been gas, sunshine, water, fungi, and plants. We have been single-celled beings. The Buddha said that in one of his former lives, he was a tree. He was a fish, he was a deer. These are not superstitious things. Every one of us has been a cloud, a deer, a bird, a fish, and we continue to be these things, not just in former lives.

This is not just the case with birth. Nothing can be born, and also nothing can die. That is what Avalokita said. Do you think that a cloud can die? To die means that from something you become nothing. Do you think that we can make something a nothing? Let us go back to our sheet of paper. We may have the illusion that to destroy it, all we have to do is light a match and burn it up. But if we burn a sheet of paper, some of it will become smoke, and the smoke will rise and continue to be. The heat that is caused by the burning paper will enter into the cosmos and penetrate other things. The heat is the next life of the paper. The ash that is formed will become part of the soil, and the sheet of paper, in his or her next life, might be a cloud and a rose at the same time. We have to be very careful and attentive in order to realize that this sheet of paper has never been born and it will never die. It can take on other forms of being, but we are not capable of transforming a sheet of paper into nothingness.

Everything is like that, even you and I. We are not subject to birth and death. A Zen master might give a student a subject of meditation like, "What was your face before your parents were born?" This is an invitation to go on a journey in order to recognize yourself. If you do well, you can see your former lives as well as your future lives. Please remember that we are not talking about philosophy; we are talking about reality. Look at your hand and ask yourself, "Since when has my hand been around?" If I look deeply into my hand I can see it has been around for a long time, hundreds of thousands of years. I see many generations of ancestors in there, not just in the past, but in the present moment, still alive. I am only the continuation. I have never died once. If I had died even once, how could my hand still be here?

The French scientist Antoine Lavoisier (1743–1794) said, "Nothing is created, and nothing is destroyed." This is exactly the same as in the Heart Sutra. Even the best contemporary scientists cannot reduce something as small as a speck of dust or an electron to nothingness. One form of energy can only become another form of energy. Something can never become nothing, and this includes a speck of dust.

Usually we say that we humans come from dust and are going back to dust, and this does not sound very joyful.

We don't want to return to dust. There is a discrimination here that humans are very valuable, and that dust has no value at all. But scientists do not even know what a speck of dust is! It is still a mystery. Imagine one atom of that speck of dust, with electrons speeding around its nucleus. It is very exciting. To return to a speck of dust will be quite an exciting adventure!

Sometimes we have the impression that we understand what a speck of dust is. We even pretend that we understand a human being—a human being who we say is going to return to dust. Because we have lived with a person for twenty or thirty years, we have the impression that we know everything about him. So, while driving in the car with that person sitting right next to us, we think about other things. We aren't interested in him anymore. What arrogance! The person sitting there beside us is really a mystery! We only have the impression that we know him, but we don't know anything yet. If we look with the eyes of Avalokita, we will see that even one hair of that person is the entire cosmos. One hair on his head can be a door opening to the ultimate reality. One speck of dust can be the Kingdom of God, the Pure Land. When you see that you, the speck of dust, and all things inter-are, you will understand that this is so. We must be humble. There is a Chinese proverb that says, "To say you don't know is the beginning of knowing."

One autumn day, I was in a park, absorbed in the contemplation of a very small but beautiful leaf in the shape of a heart. Its color was almost red, and it was barely hanging on the branch, nearly ready to fall down. I spent a long time with it, and I asked the leaf a lot of questions. I found out the leaf had been a mother to the tree. Usually we think that the tree is the mother and the leaves are just children, but as I looked at the leaf I saw that the leaf is also a mother to the tree. The sap that the roots take up is only water and minerals, not good enough to nourish the tree, so the tree distributes that sap to the leaves. The leaves take the responsibility of transforming that rough sap into refined sap and, with the help of the sun and gas, sending it back in order to nourish the tree. Therefore, the leaves are also the mother to the tree. And since the leaf is linked to the tree by a stem, the communication between them is easy to see.

We do not have a stem linking us to our mother anymore, but when we were in her womb we had a very long stem, an umbilical cord. The oxygen and the nourishment we needed came to us through that stem. Unfortunately, on the day we call our birthday, it was cut and we received the illusion that we are independent. That is a mistake. We continue to rely on our mother for a very long time, and we have several other mothers as well. The Earth is our mother. We have a great many stems linking us to our Mother Earth. There is a stem linking us with the cloud. If there is no cloud, there is no water for us to drink. We are made of at least seventy percent water; the stem between the cloud and us is really there. This is also the case with the river, the forest, the logger, and the farmer. There are hundreds of thousands of stems linking us to everything in the cosmos, and therefore we can be. Do you see the link between you and me? If you are not there, I am not here;

that is certain. If you do not see it yet, look more deeply and I am sure you will see. As I said, this is not philosophy. You really have to see.

I asked the leaf whether it was scared because it was autumn and the other leaves were falling. The leaf told me, "No. During the whole spring and summer I was very alive. I worked hard and helped nourish the tree, and much of me is in the tree. Please do not say that I am just this form, because this leaf form is only a tiny part of me. I am the whole tree. I know that I am already inside the tree, and when I go back to the soil, I will continue to nourish the tree. That's why I do not worry. As I leave this branch and float to the ground, I will wave to the tree and tell her, 'I will see you again very soon.'"

Suddenly I saw a kind of wisdom very much like the wisdom contained in the Heart Sutra. You have to *see* life. You shouldn't say, life *of* the leaf, but life *in* the leaf, and life *in* the tree. My life is just Life, and you can see it in me and in the tree. That day there was a wind blowing and, after a while, I saw the leaf leave the branch and float down to the soil, dancing joyfully, because as it floated it saw itself already there in the tree. It was so happy. I bowed my head, and I knew that we have a lot to learn from the leaf because it was not afraid—it knew that nothing can be born and nothing can die.

The cloud in the sky will also not be scared. When the time comes, the cloud will become rain. It is fun becoming rain, falling down, chanting, and becoming part of the Mississippi River, or the Amazon River, or the Mekong

River, or falling onto vegetables and later becoming part of a human being. It is a very exciting adventure. The cloud knows that if it falls to the earth it might become part of the ocean. So the cloud isn't afraid. Only humans are afraid.

A wave on the ocean has a beginning and an end, a birth and a death. But Avalokiteshvara tells us that the wave is empty. The wave is full of water, but it is empty of a separate self. A wave is a form that has been made possible, thanks to the existence of wind and water. If a wave only sees its form, with its beginning and end, it will be afraid of birth and death. But if the wave sees that it is water and identifies itself with the water, then it will be emancipated from birth and death. Each wave is born and is going to die, but the water is free from birth and death.

When I was a child I used to play with a kaleidoscope. I took a tube and a few pieces of ground glass, turned it a little bit, and saw many wonderful sights. Every time I made a small movement with my fingers, one sight would disappear and another would appear. I did not cry at all when the first spectacle disappeared, because I knew that nothing was lost. Another beautiful sight always followed. If you are the wave and you become one with the water, looking at the world with the eyes of water, then you are not afraid of going up, going down, going up, going down. But please do not be satisfied with speculation, or with taking my word for it. You have to enter it, taste it, and be one with it yourself. And that can be done through meditation, not only in the meditation hall, but throughout your daily life.

While you cook a meal, while you clean the house, while you go for a walk, you can look at things and try to see them in their nature of emptiness. Emptiness is an optimistic word; it is not at all pessimistic. When Avalokita, in his deep meditation on Perfect Understanding, was able to see the nature of emptiness, he suddenly overcame all fear and pain. I have seen people die very peacefully, with a smile, because they see that birth and death are only waves on the surface of the ocean, just the spectacle in the kaleidoscope.

So you see there are many lessons we can learn from the cloud, the water, the wave, the leaf, and the kaleidoscope—and from everything else in the cosmos, too. If you look at anything carefully and deeply enough, you discover the mystery of interbeing, and once you have seen it you will no longer be subject to fear—fear of birth, or fear of death. Birth and death are only ideas we have in our mind, and these ideas cannot be applied to reality. It is just like the idea of above and below. We are very sure that when we point our hand up, it is above, and when we point in the opposite direction, it is below. Heaven is above, and Hell is below. But the people who are sitting right now on the other side of the planet must disagree, because the idea of above and below does not apply to the cosmos, nor does the idea of birth and death.

So please continue to look back and you will see that you have always been here. Let us look together and penetrate into the life of a leaf, so we may be one with the leaf. Let us penetrate and be one with the cloud or with the wave, to realize our own nature as water and be free from our fear. If we look very deeply, we will transcend birth and death.

Tomorrow, I will continue to be. But you will have to be very attentive to see me. I will be a flower, or a leaf. I will be in these forms and I will say hello to you. If you are attentive enough, you will recognize me, and you may greet me. I will be very happy.

ROSES AND GARBAGE ~

Neither defiled nor immaculate.

Defiled or immaculate. Dirty or pure. These are concepts we form in our mind. A beautiful rose we have just cut and placed in a vase is immaculate. It smells so good, so pure, so fresh. It supports the idea of immaculateness. The opposite is a garbage can. It smells horrible, and it is filled with rotten things.

But that is only when you look on the surface. If you look more deeply you will see that in just five or six days, the rose will become part of the garbage. You do not need to wait five days to see it. If you just look at the rose, and you look deeply, you can see it now. And if you look into the garbage can, you see that in a few months its contents can be transformed into lovely vegetables, and even a rose. If you are a good organic gardener and you have the eyes of a bodhisattva, looking at a rose you can see the garbage, and looking at the garbage you can see a rose. Roses and garbage inter-are. Without a rose, we cannot have garbage; and without garbage, we cannot have a rose. They need each other very much. The rose and garbage are equal. The garbage is just as precious as the rose. If we look deeply at the concepts of defiled and immaculate, we return to the notion of interbeing.

In the Majjhima Nikaya, there is a very short passage on how the world has come to be. It is very simple, very easy to understand, and yet very deep: "This is, because that is. This is not, because that is not. This is like this, because that is like that." This is the Buddhist teaching of Genesis.

In the city of Manila there are many young prostitutes, some of them only fourteen or fifteen years old. They are very unhappy young people. They did not want to be prostitutes. Their families are poor and these young girls went to the city to look for some kind of job, like a street vendor, to make money to send back to their families. Of course this is not true only in Manila, but in Ho Chi Minh City in Vietnam, in Lagos in Nigeria, in New York City, and in Paris also. It is true that in the city you can make money more easily than in the countryside, so we can imagine how a young girl may have been tempted to go there to help her family. But after only a few weeks there, she was persuaded by a clever person to work for her and to earn perhaps one hundred times more money. Because she was so young and did not know much about life, she accepted and became a prostitute. Since that time, she has carried the feeling of being impure, defiled, and this causes her great suffering. When she looks at other young girls, dressed beautifully, belonging to good families, a wretched feeling wells up in her, and this feeling of defilement has become her hell.

But if she had an opportunity to meet with Avalokita, he would tell her to look deeply at herself and at the whole situation, and see that she is like this because other people are like that. "This is like this, because that is like that." So how can a so-called good girl, belonging to a good family, be proud? Because their way of life is like this, the other girl has to be like that. No one among us has clean hands. No one of us can claim it is not our responsibility. The girl in Manila is that way because of the way we are. Looking into the life of that young prostitute, we see the people who are not prostitutes. And looking at the people who are not prostitutes, and at the way we live our lives, we see the prostitute. This helps to create that, and that helps to create this.

Let us look at wealth and poverty. The affluent society and the society that is deprived of everything inter-are. The wealth of one society is made of the poverty of the other. "This is like this, because that is like that." Wealth is made of non-wealth elements, and poverty is made of non-poverty elements. It is exactly the same as with the sheet of paper. So we must be careful. We should not imprison ourselves in concepts. The truth is that everything is everything else. We can only inter-be, we cannot just be. And we are responsible for everything that happens around us. Avalokiteshvara would tell the young prostitute, "My child, look at yourself and you will see everything. Because other people are like that, you are like this. You are not the only person who is responsible, so please do not suffer." Only by seeing with the eyes of interbeing can that young girl be freed from her suffering. What else can you offer her to help her be free?

We are imprisoned by our ideas of good and evil. We want to be only good, and we want to remove all evil. But that is because we forget that good is made of non-good elements. Suppose I am holding a lovely branch. When we look at it with a nondiscriminating mind, we see this wonderful branch. But as soon as we distinguish that one end is the left and the other end is the right, we get into trouble. We may say we want only the left, and we do not want the right (as you hear very often), and there is trouble right away. If the rightist is not there, how can you be a leftist? Let us say that I do not want the right end of this branch, that I only want the left. So, I break off half of this reality and throw it away. But as soon as I throw the unwanted half away, the end that remains becomes the new right. Because as soon as the left is there, the right must be there also. If I become frustrated and do it again, breaking what remains of my branch in half, I will still have a right and a left.

The same may be applied to good and evil. You cannot be good alone. You cannot hope to remove evil, because thanks to evil, good exists, and vice versa. When you stage a play about a heroic figure, you have to provide an antagonist in order for the hero to be a hero. So, Buddha needs Mara to take the evil role so Buddha can be a buddha. Buddha is as empty as the sheet of paper; Buddha is made of non-Buddha elements. If non-buddhas like us are not here, how can a buddha be? If the rightist is not there, how can there be a leftist?

In my tradition, every time I join my palms together to make a deep bow to the Buddha, I chant this short verse:

The one who bows and the one who is bowed to
are both, by nature, empty.
Therefore the communication between us
is inexpressibly perfect.

It is not arrogant to say so. If I am not empty, how can I bow down to the Buddha? And if the Buddha is not empty, how can he receive my bow? The Buddha and I inter-are. Buddha is made of non-Buddha elements, like me. And I am made of non-me elements, like the Buddha. So the subject and object of reverence are both empty. Without an object, how can a subject exist?

In the West you have been struggling for many years with the problem of evil. How is it possible that evil should be there? It seems to be difficult for the Western mind to understand. But in the light of nonduality, there is no problem: As soon as the idea of good is there, the idea of evil is there. Buddha needs Mara in order to reveal himself, and vice versa. When you perceive reality in this way, you will not discriminate against the garbage in favor of the rose. You will cherish both. You need both right and left in order to have a branch. Do not take sides. If you take sides, you are trying to eliminate half of reality, which is impossible. For many years, the United States has been trying to describe various other countries as evil, from North Vietnam to the former Soviet Union, to Iran, Iraq, and North Korea. Some Americans even have the illusion that they can survive alone, without these other countries. Other countries may believe that they, too, can exist without us. The American imperialists, they might say, are on the bad side and must be eliminated for happiness to be possible. But that is the dualistic way of looking at things. It is the same as believing that the right side can exist without the left side.

If we look at the U.S. very deeply, we see Iran. And if we look deeply at Iran, we see the U.S. If we look deeply at the rose, we see the garbage; if we look deeply at the garbage, we see the rose. In international politics, each side pretends to be the rose and calls the other side the garbage. Recently, a young person asked me: "Why do we give different names to different things, since they're really together, they're really one?" That's a very good question. I replied: "That's the root of problems—names, the fact that we give names to everything. We give places different names, like America, Iran, Iraq. But in fact they all belong to the earth; they shouldn't fight each other. Israel and Palestine are two hands of the same body. They continue to suffer because they haven't touched the wisdom of nondiscrimination that they have inside them."

Clearly, "this is, because that is." You have to work for the survival of the other side if you want to survive yourself. It is really very simple. Survival means the survival of humankind as a whole, not just a part of it. And we know now that this must be realized not only between the United States and the Middle East, but also between the East and West, the North and South. If the South cannot survive, then the North is going to crumble. If developing countries cannot pay their debts, everyone will suffer. If we do not take care of poorer countries, the well-being of richer countries is not going to last, and we will not be able to continue living in the way we have been for much longer. Only when we can touch the wisdom of nondiscrimination in us can we all survive.

So do not hope that you can eliminate the evil side. It is easy to think that we are on the good side, and that the other side is evil. But wealth is made of poverty, and poverty is made of wealth. This is a very clear vision of reality. We do not have to look far to see what we have to do. The citizens of every country are human beings. We cannot study and understand a human being just through statistics. You can't leave the job to the governments or the political scientists alone. You have to do it yourself. If you arrive at an understanding of the fears and hopes of a citizen from Iraq or Sudan or Afghanistan, then you can understand your own fears and hopes. Only penetration into reality can save us. Fear cannot save us.

We are not separate. We are inextricably inter-related. The rose is the garbage, and the non-prostitute is the prostitute. The rich man is the very poor woman, and the Buddhist is the non-Buddhist. The non-Buddhist cannot help but be a Buddhist, because we inter-are. The emancipation of the young prostitute will come as she sees into the nature of interbeing. She will know that she is bearing the fruit of the whole world. And if we look into ourselves and see her, we bear her pain, and the pain of the whole world.

THE MOON IS ALWAYS
THE MOON ~

Neither increasing nor decreasing.

We worry because we think that, after we die, we will not be a human being anymore. We will go back to being a speck of dust. We think we will be somehow diminished.

But that is not true. A speck of dust contains the whole universe. If we were as big as the sun, we might look down at the Earth and see it as insignificant. As human beings, we look at dust in the same way. But the ideas of big and small are just concepts in our minds. Everything contains everything else; that is the principle of interpenetration. This sheet of paper contains the sunshine, the logger, the forest, everything, so the idea that a sheet of paper is small or insignificant is just an idea. We cannot destroy even one sheet of paper. We are incapable of destroying anything. Those who assassinated Mahatma Gandhi and Martin Luther King, Jr. hoped to reduce them to nothingness. But these people continue to be with us, perhaps even more than before, because they continue in other forms. We, ourselves, continue their being. So let us not be afraid of diminishing. We are like the moon. We see the moon waxing and waning, but it is always the moon.

BUDDHA IS MADE OF
NON-BUDDHA ELEMENTS ~

Therefore in emptiness there is neither form, nor feelings, nor
*   perceptions,*
nor mental formations, nor consciousness.
No eye, or ear, or nose, or tongue, or body, or mind.
No form, no sound, no smell, no taste, no touch, no object of mind.
No realms of elements (from eyes to mind consciousness),
no interdependent origins and no extinction of them
(from ignorance to death and decay).
No ill-being, no cause of ill-being, no end of ill-being, and no path.
No understanding and no attainment.

The first sentence is a confirmation that the five skandhas are all empty. They cannot exist by themselves.
Each one has to inter-be with all the other skandhas.

The next part of the verse is an enumeration of the
eighteen realms of elements (*dhatus*). First we have the
six sense organs: eyes, ears, nose, tongue, body, and mind.
Then there are the six sense objects: form, sound, smell,
taste, touch, and object of mind. Form is the object of eyes,
sound is the object of ears, and so on. Finally, the contact
between these first twelve brings about the six conscious-
nesses: sight, hearing, smell, taste, touch, and the last is mind

consciousness. So, with eyes as the first realm of elements and mind consciousness as the eighteenth, this part of the sutra is saying that not one of these realms can exist by itself, because each can only inter-be with every other realm.

The next part speaks of the twelve interdependent origins (*pratitya samutpada*), which begin with ignorance and end with old age and death. The meaning in the sutra is that none of these twelve can exist by itself. Each must rely on the being of the others in order for it to be. Therefore, all of them are empty, and because they are empty, they really exist. The same principle applies to the Four Noble Truths: "No ill-being, no cause of ill-being, no end of ill-being, and no path." The last line in this section is: "No understanding and no attainment." Understanding (prajña) is the essence of a Buddha. "No understanding" means understanding has no separate existence. Understanding is made of non-understanding elements, just as Buddha is made of non-Buddha elements.

I want to tell you a story about Buddha and Mara. One day the Buddha was in his cave, and Ananda, who was the Buddha's attendant, was standing outside near the door. Suddenly Ananda saw Mara coming. He was surprised. He didn't want that, and he wished Mara would get lost. But Mara walked straight up to Ananda and asked him to announce his visit to the Buddha.

Ananda said, "Why have you come here? Don't you remember that long ago you were defeated by the Buddha under the bodhi tree? Aren't you ashamed to come here?

Go away! The Buddha will not see you. You are evil. You are his enemy."

When Mara heard this, he began to laugh and laugh. "Did you say your teacher told you he has enemies?" That made Ananda very embarrassed. He knew that his teacher had not said that he has enemies. So Ananda was defeated and had to go in and announce Mara, hoping that the Buddha would say, "Go and tell him that I am not here. Tell him that I am in a meeting."

But the Buddha was very excited when he heard that Mara, such a very old friend, had come to visit him. "Is that true? Is he really here?" the Buddha said, and he went out in person to greet Mara. Ananda was distressed. The Buddha went right up to Mara, bowed to him, and took his hands in his in the warmest way. The Buddha said, "Hello! How are you? How have you been? Is everything all right?"

Mara didn't say anything. So the Buddha brought him into the cave, prepared a seat for him to sit down, and told Ananda to go and make herb tea for both of them. "I can make tea for my master one hundred times a day, but making tea for Mara is not a joy," Ananda thought to himself. But since this was the order of his master, how could he refuse? So Ananda went to prepare some herb tea for the Buddha and his so-called guest, but while doing this he tried to listen to their conversation.

The Buddha repeated very warmly, "How have you been? How are things with you?" Mara said, "Things are not going well at all. I am tired of being a Mara. I want to be something else."

Ananda became very frightened. Mara said, "You know, being a Mara is not a very easy thing to do. If you talk, you have to talk in riddles. If you do anything, you have to be tricky and look evil. I am very tired of all that. But what I cannot bear is my disciples. They are now talking about social justice, peace, equality, liberation, nonduality, nonviolence, all of that. I have had enough of it! I think that it would be better if I hand them all over to you. I want to be something else."

Ananda began to shudder because he was afraid that the master would decide to take the other role. Mara would become the Buddha, and the Buddha would become Mara. It made him very sad.

The Buddha listened attentively and was filled with compassion. Finally, he said in a quiet voice, "Do you think it's fun being a Buddha? You don't know what my disciples have done to me! They put words into my mouth that I never said. They build garish temples and put statues of me on altars in order to attract bananas and oranges and sweet rice, just for themselves. And they package me and make my teaching into an item of commerce. Mara, if you knew what it is really like to be a Buddha, I am sure you wouldn't want to be one." And, thereupon, the Buddha recited a long verse summarizing the conversation.

FREEDOM ~

"Because there is no attainment,
the Bodhisattvas, grounded in Perfect Understanding,
find no obstacles for their minds.
Having no obstacles, they overcome fear,
liberating themselves forever from illusion and realizing perfect
Nirvana.
All Buddhas in the past, present, and future,
thanks to this Perfect Understanding,
arrive at full, right, and universal Enlightenment.

Obstacles are our ideas and concepts concerning birth and death, defilement, immaculateness, increasing, decreasing, above, below, inside, outside, Buddha, Mara, and so on. Once we see with the eyes of interbeing, these obstacles are removed from our mind and we overcome fear, liberating ourselves forever from illusion, and realizing perfect Nirvana. Once the wave realizes that it is only water, that it is nothing but water, it realizes that birth and death cannot do it any harm. It has transcended all kinds of fear, and perfect Nirvana is the state of non-fear. You are liberated, you are no longer subject to birth and death, defilement and immaculateness. You are free from all that.

SVAHA! ~

"Therefore, one should know
that Perfect Understanding is the highest mantra, the
    unequalled mantra,
the destroyer of ill-being, the incorruptible truth.
A mantra of Prajñaparamita should therefore be proclaimed:
Gate gate paragate parasamgate bodhi svaha."

A mantra is something that you utter when your body, your mind, and your breath are at one in deep concentration. When you dwell in that deep concentration, you look into things and see them as clearly as you see an orange that you hold in the palm of your hand. Looking deeply into the five skandhas, Avalokiteshvara saw the nature of interbeing and overcame all pain. He became completely liberated. It was in that state of deep concentration, of joy, of liberation, that he uttered something important. That is why his utterance is a mantra.

When two young people love each other, but one of them has not said so yet, the other person may be waiting for three very important words. If the first person is a very responsible person, he probably wants to be sure of his feeling, and he may wait a long time before saying it. Then one day, sitting together in a park, when no one else is nearby and everything is quiet, after the two of them have been silent for a long time, he utters these three words. When the second person hears this, she trembles, because it is such an important statement. When you say something like that with your whole being, not just with your mouth or your intellect, but with your whole being, it can transform the world. A statement that has such power of transformation is called a mantra.

Avalokiteshvara's mantra is "*Gate gate paragate parasam-gate bodhi svaha.*" *Gate* means gone. Gone from suffering to the liberation from suffering. Gone from forgetfulness to mindfulness. Gone from duality into nonduality. *Gate gate* means gone, gone. *Paragate* means gone all the way to the other shore. So this mantra is said in a very strong way. Gone, gone, gone all the way over. In *parasamgate, sam* means everyone, the Sangha, the entire community of beings. Everyone gone over to the other shore. *Bodhi* is the light inside, enlightenment, or awakening. You see it and the vision of reality liberates you. And *svaha* is a cry of joy or excitement, like "ah!" or "hurrah!" or "hallelujah!" "Gone, gone, gone all the way over, everyone gone to the other shore, enlightenment!"

That is what the bodhisattva uttered. When we listen to this mantra, we should bring ourselves into that state of attention and concentration, so that we can receive the strength emanated by Avalokiteshvara Bodhisattva. We do not recite the Heart Sutra like singing a song, or with our intellect alone. If you practice the meditation on empti-ness, if you penetrate the nature of interbeing with all your heart, your body, and your mind, you will realize a state that is quite concentrated. If you say the mantra then, with all your being, the mantra will have power and you will be able to have real communication, real communion with Avalokiteshvara, and you will be able to transform yourself in the direction of enlightenment. This text is not just for chanting, or to be put on an altar for worship. It is given to us as a tool to work for our liberation, for the liberation of all beings. It is like a tool for farming, given to us so that we may farm. This is the gift of Avalokita.

There are three kinds of gifts. The first is the gift of material resources. The second is the gift of knowledge, the gift of the Dharma. The third, the highest kind of gift, is the gift of non-fear. Avalokiteshvara Bodhisattva is someone who can help us liberate ourselves from fear. This is the heart of the Prajñaparamita.

A TANGERINE PARTY ～

The Prajñaparamita gives us solid ground for making peace with ourselves, for transcending the fear of birth and death, the duality of this and that. In the light of emptiness, everything is everything else, we inter-are, everyone is responsible for everything that happens in life. When you produce peace and happiness in yourself, you begin to realize peace for the whole world. With the smile that you produce in yourself, with the conscious breathing you establish within yourself, you begin to work for peace in the world. To smile is not to smile only for yourself; the world will change because of your smile. When you practice sitting meditation, if you enjoy even one moment of your sitting, if you establish serenity and happiness inside yourself, you provide the world with a solid base of peace. If you do not give yourself peace, how can you share it with others? If you do not begin your peace work with yourself, where will you go to begin it? To sit, to smile, to look at things and really see them, these are the basis of peace work

Sometimes at Deer Park we have a tangerine party. Everyone is offered one tangerine. We put the tangerine in the palm of our hand and look at it, breathing in a way that the tangerine becomes real. Most of the time when we eat a tangerine, we do not look at it. We think about many other things. To look at a tangerine is to see the blossom forming into the fruit, to see the sunshine and the rain. The tangerine in our palm is the wonderful presence of life. We are able to really see that tangerine and smell its blossom and the warm, moist earth. As the tangerine becomes real, we become real. Life in that moment becomes real.

Mindfully, we peel our tangerine and smell its fragrance. We carefully take each section of the tangerine and put it on our tongue, and we can feel that it is a real tangerine. We eat each section of the tangerine in perfect mindfulness until we finish the entire fruit. Eating a tangerine in this way is very important, because both the tangerine and the eater of the tangerine become real. This, too, is the basic work for peace.

In Buddhist meditation we do not struggle for the kind of enlightenment that will happen five or ten years from now. We practice so that each moment of our life becomes real life. And, therefore, when we meditate, we sit just for sitting; we don't sit for something else. If we sit for twenty minutes, these twenty minutes should bring us joy, life. If we practice walking meditation, we walk just for walking, not to arrive anywhere. We have to be alive with each step, and if we are, each step brings real life back to us.

The same kind of mindfulness can be practiced when we eat breakfast, or when we hold a child in our arms. Hugging is a Western custom, but we from the East would like to contribute the practice of conscious breathing to it. When you hold a child in your arms, or hug your mother, or your husband, or your friend, breathe in and out three times and your happiness will be multiplied at least tenfold.

And when you look at someone, really look at them with mindfulness and practice conscious breathing.

At the beginning of each meal, I recommend that you look at your bowl and silently recite, "My bowl is empty now, but I know that it is going to be filled with delicious food in just a moment." While waiting to be served or to serve yourself, I suggest you breathe three times and look at your bowl even more deeply, "At this very moment many, many people around the world are also holding a bowl, but their bowl is going to be empty for a long time." Over forty thousand children die each day because of malnutrition. And that is only the children. We can be very happy to have such wonderful food, but we also suffer because we are capable of seeing. When we see in this way, it makes us sane, because the way in front of us—the way to live so that we can make peace with ourselves and with the world—is clear. When we see the good and the bad, the wondrous and the deep suffering, we have to live in a way that we can make peace between ourselves and the world. Understanding is the fruit of meditation. Understanding is the basis of everything.

Each breath we take, each step we make, each smile we realize, is a positive contribution to peace, a necessary step in the direction of peace for the world. In the light of interbeing, peace and happiness in your daily life means peace and happiness in the world.

Thank you for being so attentive. Thank you for listening to Avalokiteshvara. Because you are there, the Heart Sutra has become very easy.

PARALLAX PRESS, a nonprofit organization, publishes books on engaged Buddhism and the practice of mindfulness by Thich Nhat Hanh and other authors. All of Thich Nhat Hanh's work is available at our online store and in our free catalog. For a copy of the catalog, please contact:

PARALLAX PRESS
P.O. Box 7355
Berkeley, CA 94707
www.parallax.org

Monastics and laypeople practice the art of mindful living in the tradition of Thich Nhat Hanh at retreat communities in France and the United States. To reach any of these communities, or for information about individuals and families joining for a practice period, please contact:

PLUM VILLAGE
13 Martineau
33580 Dieulivol, France
www.plumvillage.org

BLUE CLIFF MONASTERY
3 Mindfulness Road
Pine Bush, NY 12566
www.bluecliffmonastery.org

DEER PARK MONASTERY
2499 Melru Lane
Escondido, CA 92026
www.deerparkmonastery.org

The Mindfulness Bell, a journal of the art of mindful living in the tradition of Thich Nhat Hanh, is published three times a year by Plum Village. To subscribe or to see the worldwide directory of Sanghas, visit www.mindfulnessbell.org.

RELATED TITLES BY THICH NHAT HANH